Color Palettes

CLARKSON POTTER / PUBLISHERS   NEW YORK

Text by JACQUELINE GOEWEY   *Additional photography by* FERNANDO BENGOECHEA

Color Palettes

ATMOSPHERIC INTERIORS USING THE DONALD KAUFMAN COLOR COLLECTION

By Suzanne Butterfield *Major photography by* PETER MARGONELLI

Copyright © 1998 by Suzanne Butterfield
Photographs copyright © 1998 by Peter Margonelli
Title page photograph copyright © 1998 by Alan Richardson
Photographs on the following pages copyright © 1998 by
Fernando Bengoechea: 10, 14, 23, 25, 26, 27, 28, 29, 31, 32, 34, 35,
36, 37, 38, 61, 62, 63, 64, 65, 81, 105, 106, 107, 108, 109

Published by Clarkson N. Potter, Inc., 201 East 50th Street,
New York, New York 10022. Member of the Crown Publishing Group.

Random House, Inc. New York, Toronto, London, Sydney, Auckland
http://www.randomhouse.com/

CLARKSON N. POTTER, POTTER, and colophon
are trademarks of Clarkson N. Potter, Inc.

Printed in Japan

Design by Douglas Turshen

Library of Congress Cataloging-in-Publication Data
Butterfield, Suzanne
    Color palettes: by Suzanne Butterfield; principal photography
by Peter Margonelli; additional photography by Fernando Bengoechea;
text by Jacqueline Goewey.—1st ed.
    1. Color in interior decoration.   2. Interior walls.
I. Kaufman, Donald.   II. Goewey, Jacqueline.   III. Title.
NK2115.5.C6B88   1998
747'.94—dc21   97-20914

ISBN 0-609-60144-X

10 9 8 7 6 5 4 3 2

I WANT TO THANK Donald Kaufman and Taffy Dahl for so many generous and important contributions to this project. I am grateful for their insight and support. It is always an inspiration to explore the subject of color with them and I have enjoyed our collaboration and partnership over the years.

I also wish to express appreciation to my editor, Carol Southern, a color enthusiast at heart, who has been a source of encouragement from our very first meeting and a perceptive and invaluable advisor.

Special thanks to Peter Margonelli. Thanks also to Doug Turshen for his design, to his able assistant Nora Negron, to Rochelle Udell for all the hours of inspired painting with Donald Kaufman colors, to Jane Treuhaft for sorting out the details with such a careful eye, and to Mark McCauslin, Joan Denman, and all the others at Clarkson Potter who helped bring this book to fruition.

Others I would like to thank for their individual contributions: Jacqueline Goewey, Fernando Bengoechea, Alexandra Enders, Matt Petosa, Chris Cozzarin, Joe Pisarri, Greg George, and the whole crew at The Color Factory. In addition, I am grateful to everyone who opened their homes and allowed us to photograph the palettes they created.

Most important, I thank Stuart, Emmelyn, and Helen for their endless patience.

acknowledgments

contents

foreword

AS AN ART STUDENT, a teacher, and a painter, I spent many years in the classroom and studio dealing with colors and experiencing what happens to them when they are mixed. When I taught painting, I advised students to mix colors the way I had been taught, using complements: red to subdue green, violet to gray-off yellow, blue to soften orange. This was how a color could become grayer without becoming dead. Using complements to preserve a color's luminosity while adjusting its intensity is standard practice among artists.

During summers, when I took jobs as a part-time housepainter, I was surprised to find that painters and paint stores avoided mixing complements. Adding red to green, for instance, was thought to make things too complicated, and colors too hard to match.

Later, I learned there is a worldwide system of color mixing in place, set up to avoid complements and arrive at paint colors by a simpler method. This practice has facilitated industrial color matching beautifully, but left architectural color without the benefit of the richness complements can provide. Acting on this realization, I began mixing my house paint colors with their complements and then with sets of complements to add up to a full spectrum of color in each can. This not only made the hue richer in a small sample, but caused the color on the wall to reflect light more efficiently, reacting to its constant changes as it shifts throughout the day. I found this also worked well for interiors. The same luminous quality experienced outdoors in nature could be created indoors, making the room and the things in it more natural.

When my wife, Taffy Dahl, became my partner, we began developing a method for painting interiors with these full-spectrum colors, working collaboratively with architects, designers, and private clients. We came to understand how individual full-spectrum colors could be enhanced by using them in combination, and how the light reflected by these full-spectrum colors enriched the colors of everything else in the space.

Suzanne Butterfield, a retailing professional, recognized this dimension to our paint and helped us spread the word. Eventually, we collaborated on our first book, *Color: Natural Palettes for Painted Rooms,* and introduced our own line of thirty colors, The Donald Kaufman Collection. Since we had, up to that point, only made custom colors for specific sites, we worked hard, asking the opinion of many designers to establish a range that could be useful for a variety of purposes and decorating styles.

In this book, Suzanne has undertaken the task of documenting a range of projects employing our colors and a few more we felt should be included to enhance the collection. We trust that these painted rooms will serve not only to inspire, but to provide a framework for bringing some method and order to the often daunting process of selecting colors for interiors.

DONALD KAUFMAN
NEW YORK CITY, MARCH 1997

introduction

CLASSICAL PROPORTIONS, light streaming through windows, the patina of old wood floors, the smooth marble of a mantel: Many elements go into making a beautiful room. One of the most important is color; certainly it is the one we can most easily control, often with profound results. The effect of painting a room is far greater than simply coloring the walls. The color interacts with light and all the other elements in a setting to create an atmosphere. This in turn has direct bearing on something intangible yet real: how we feel when we're in the room. This atmosphere can be extraordinarily versatile, from a bedroom's warm yellow to a dining room's dramatic red, from a hall's unobtrusive taupe to a sunny living room's shimmering whites. Strategic use of color can mask structural difficulties and highlight architectural triumphs, celebrate the character of a place, compensate for its weaknesses.

Most of us know the colors we like and whether or not we feel comfortable in an environment. But deciding which colors fit our own space—which colors will make the room feel just right—can be intimidating. Where should one start? Just as there is never a single perfect color for a room, there is never only one correct place to start. Coming to informed conclusions about coloring a room is a process, not a step-by-step program. Before determining actual hues, you'll need to think about the nature of your space, its virtues and flaws. By focusing on different aspects of the space, you'll gather important information about the character of the rooms, the architectural features, and the quality of light. And you will continually come back to two fundamental questions: How do I use the room and what should the space feel like as a whole?

One very helpful approach is to visualize a space in terms of its "broad planes"

—the walls, ceiling, and floor. The color atmosphere of a room results not only from whatever hue is on the walls, but from how the walls interact with the ceiling and the floor, with the light coming in through the windows (which, of course, is constantly changing), and with glimpses of other rooms seen through doorways. We tend to focus consciously on the details of a room—the flowers in the vase, the velvet sofa, the pale blue silk curtains—but the color of a room, the atmosphere that we absorb, is actually established by the simple planes of ceiling, walls, and floor.

A word about floors. Most people tend to think of color in terms of paint, fabric, and carpet. Too often they skip over the color of a wood floor, dismissing it as just "wood." In fact, the color and nature of the floor are important elements in establishing atmosphere. And as the surface that often receives the most direct light, the floor can be a greater reflecting factor than any other surface in the same area.

Just as you look to the broad planes in a room, it is important to consider not only a single room at a time (unless you have just one), but a series of rooms—to see the living room in relation to the dining room and the front hall, the bedroom connected to the study, and so forth. People often forget to think of color choices in terms of a sequence. In reality, rooms are seen from one to the other, and the interplay of colors between rooms is as important as the colors for individual rooms; elements within rooms and what surrounds them all affect color atmosphere.

Once you've established the broad strokes (i.e., walls before baseboard), you can go back and look at the specific details. Was there an element that particularly attracted you to the space? A beautiful crown molding? A grand skylight? Floor-to-ceiling mahogany bookcases? Incredible views? If you are lucky enough to have an interior with a defining gesture or distinctive attribute that feels particularly important, you will probably wish to base many of your decisions around it.

The amount of light that comes into the apartment or house will affect the color sequence. What is the relative amount of light in any given room? Which is the lightest and which is the darkest room? The character and brightness of the light is also crucial. A warm, direct southern exposure will differ dramatically from a cooler, indirect northern exposure.

What will be the major source of light at the time the rooms are most occupied? Whether you rely on daylight, artificial lighting, or candlelight will affect your color choices. If a room is bathed in sunlight during the hours you use it most, then the palest tints and whites can be enjoyed. On the other hand, a light color will never come to life in a dark room. But a rich, deep color can make a dim, somber space feel warm and luminous, even though it receives no natural light. Windows are an important feature of every room: The amount of light they yield determines what you have to work with. The more light you have, the greater the flexibility.

Other factors also affect the quality of light and have an impact on a room's atmosphere. Where does the light come from? Not all light comes directly from the sky—there could be a reflecting body of water outside or a glaring white or brick red building across the way. A ground-floor room will probably have reflections from the sidewalk. Does the light come directly in or is it filtered in some way, through window treatments on the inside or foliage on the outside? For example, if you have gauzy cream-colored curtains, the light will have a warm cast; if there are trees outside, then half the year the light in the room will have a greenish cast.

While considering all of these questions, you need to balance practical issues—what is actually there—with what you wish the place to be. This will be a combination of what pleases you and how you will use the rooms. Are they inhabited mainly at night or during the day? Are they for working, entertaining, or relaxing? For the display of a collection? For lingering in or as passageway to other areas? How you intend to live in a space is one of the most important aspects of the whole process.

Once you know your space, you can imagine specific colors filling your rooms. The right color choice is a personal matter, and in general finding color hues—the literal colors—is not as important as finding color values and temperatures. (Values are lights and darks—what you would observe in a black-and-white photograph of your room; temperature is how warm or cool the color feels.) The interplay between opposing values and temperatures provides contrasts, and contrasts—whether subtle or strong—are an inherent part of a successful visual picture, which every space needs to feel complete.

The greater the contrast, the more the eye is attracted. You can quite literally control where the eye goes by controlling the contrasts with other rooms. If the walls and ceilings meet with beautifully detailed moldings, highlighting them with bold contrasts is appropriate; on the other hand, a very ordinary wall-ceiling meeting can be downplayed with less contrast. The same principle applies to windows and doorways, and between rooms.

We respond to color on different levels—the eye picks up relationships that the conscious mind might not be aware of. By contrasting, or complementing, warm colors, such as yellow or red, with their cool counterparts, such as blue or green, we can intensify each color and also manipulate how we perceive a space. A yellow room will appear all the more warm and luminous (and yellow) if the trim contains tints of blue. Painting the adjoining hall a cool gray will reinforce the warmth of the yellow room—and the coolness of the hall. And since our eye is always drawn to a luminous source, we will be pulled out of the transitional hall space and into the inviting yellow room.

Contrasts can be a never ending game of where you take the eye in a space. Rooms of similar colors meld while rooms painted in different colors seem to take up more space. For instance, painting a small collection of rooms all one color can make the total space seem smaller, while using varied colors can give it the semblance of different environments. Also, neighboring volumes of color have significant impact on one another and provide opportunities to control our perception of a space by combining complementing, contrasting, and opposing colors.

As you go about planning color atmospheres for your rooms, start with one color and decide each time why you need an additional one. Having a reason for everything you do will help you select colors that follow a natural progression of decisions appropriate for your space. Each room or space should contain at least a small amount of red, yellow, and blue, even if all the tones are neutral. It's possible to have whites that are bluish or yellowish and beiges that are reddish. Using the three primary colors in some form—a painted ceiling, a carpet, the trim on the curtains, or a collection of objects—will create harmony and visual balance. By the same token, using full-spectrum paints in which each color contains at least a modicum of blue, yellow, and red will enhance the results. The way light interacts with the colors will be much more complex, subtle, and luminous.

The following pages illustrate common situations in many architectural styles. Working with color is an inspiring process of discovery: The unending possibilities for contrasts between light and dark, between complements and warm and cool colors, allow you to create an infinite range of satisfying interior atmospheres.

intensity

a strong

Saturated colors emphasize strong architectural lines,
matching the impact of bold furniture and art.

statement

A PALETTE OF DIVERSE colors works to great effect in a turn-of-the-century carriage house owned by two artists. The larger-than-life setting, composed of overscaled rooms with exposed beams around a triple-height stairwell, is furnished with the owners' collection of bold paintings, photographs, and sculptures. Since the total environment—from architecture to objects—makes such a strong statement, the background colors can afford to be just as bold, so walls have been painted in very strong colors—from pumpkin orange to Prussian blue.

The central hall and soaring stairwell are colored a bright citrus yellow, acting as the natural centerpiece of the house. Yellow, found at the center of the spectrum and the color most evocative of sunlight, creates a luminous core forming the backbone for the entire house. Trim colors throughout the house delineate the spaces. Trim in the stairwell is painted a deep blue-green, complementing the yellow walls, while trim in all the surrounding rooms is painted the same deep brick red as the exterior of the house. Pulling this deep red inside—most dramatically seen in the window frames—not only gives more visual weight to the bold lines of the building but emphatically links these rooms to the outside architecture. The color system allows the red trim to visually ground the perimeter rooms, while emphasizing the soaring quality of the central hall.

Rooms surrounding the hall are painted in rich, vibrant hues. All are strong colors, so that none domi-

The living room, painted the color of a manila envelope, is less vibrant than other rooms, signaling its use as a space for relaxing. PREVIOUS PAGE: Yellow walls seem appropriate for the central hall, since it is the hue found at the center of the spectrum. Openings between rooms provide glimpses of other spaces; the resulting landscape of color illustrates the energy of complementary and contrasting hues.

nates, visually linked with the brick red trim. Two main rooms open symmetrically on either side of the great hall. The living room walls are deep cream—the color of a manila envelope—and create a warm, glowing atmosphere; the same color is used with the brick red in the bold diamond-patterned floor. The dining room, with floors of bright orange pine, is painted a brilliant squash color, and is also trimmed in the brick red. All the surfaces in this room are intensely warm, creating a visual contrast with cooler colors seen in the distance (like the green trim in the stairwell). Vistas created between the center area and the perimeter rooms are especially significant, as the colors interact—to relieve or enhance one another, completing the spectrum and enabling this eclectic mix of furniture, art, and color to work so effectively.

"Truth" wallpaper in the
back stair hallway (OPPOSITE,
ABOVE) was designed
by owner Helene Verin. Deep
blue-green trim acts as
a potent complement to the
bright citrus walls of the
three-story central stairway.
Suspended in the upstairs
landing (LEFT) is a steel
sculpture by Berkshire artist
Joey Wheaton.

In the living room (OPPOSITE,
BELOW), a collection of bold
colors achieves a kind of
serenity. In this mix of strong
elements—from the lines
of the beams and doors to
the vibrant paintings by owner
Rodney Ripps—no one thing
dominates, and yet nothing
is obscured. Complementary
blues and yellows in a collection of old clock paintings
in the bathroom (RIGHT) are
reflected in the palette
of the walls, trim, and floor.

vibrant

A brilliant terra-cotta hall sets up an interplay of intense warm and
cool contrasts, providing a foil for graphic black and white elements.

contrasts

SOMETIMES ONE INTENSE color is strong enough to form the foundation of a palette—to be the grand gesture against which everything else is measured. In this early 1840 house in Hudson, New York, the center hall is painted a brilliant terra-cotta. The eye-catching color was decided on, in part, to balance the impact of the graphic black and white tiled floor. But the color's influence extends even beyond the entry hall. Because it is located squarely in the middle of the house, the vibrant terra-cotta walls affect the palette of all the surrounding rooms.

Wall colors of some nearby rooms match the center hall in strength. The living room, for example, is painted in a graphite gray, a strong, cool color in contrast to the warmth of the hall, the equal of the hall's terra-cotta in intensity. And since the hallway can be seen through the living room doorways, its influence is constantly felt. The two wall colors have a powerful effect on each other, their juxtaposition of warm and cool pushing each to its opposite extreme. In fact, looking back to the hall, the deeply saturated gray walls make the vibrant terra-cotta appear even more intense, much like the glow of

The graphite-colored walls of the living room (RIGHT) are of equal intensity to the terra-cotta of the hall (PREVIOUS PAGE). The juxtaposition of the two rooms provides a strong visual contrast of warm and cool spaces, while the white-painted trim links them. Black and white furniture and objects appear as silhouettes against these strong backdrops.

a fire seems warmer and redder when the rest of the room is in shadow. The cool gray walls of the room also cause the yellow tones of the natural pine floors and sisal carpet to feel warmer in contrast, adding reassuring golden hues to the room.

In the dining room, walls are colored a paler gray than in the living room, for this room is removed from the influence of the hall's vibrant color. Since the geometric pattern of the floor is continued here but in a more subdued palette of gray and cream, the gray was modulated to a lighter hue in response to it. And as light gray walls meet this subtly colored floor, the contrast between the two is lessened; the edges appear softer, creating the illusion of a misty atmosphere. The filmy gray also echoes the diffused quality of the sunlight, which streams in through tall French doors, filtered by the greenery and the huge trees in the adjacent garden.

Throughout the house, owned by artist Frank Faulkner, there is an interplay of intensities, with some rooms matching the hall in strength, others providing a respite. Crisp white trim provides a clean counterpoint to highlight each wall color and also visually unites the rooms as one moves from the dynamic hallway to the more serene living spaces.

In a white bedroom (OPPOSITE), **cream trim forms a softer contrast, creating a more neutral frame from which to view the vibrant hall. The gray floor in the upstairs hall landing** (ABOVE RIGHT) **is a less dramatic partner to the terra-cotta walls than the diamond-patterned floor downstairs.**

In the dining room, removed from the intensely colored hall, walls are a paler gray. The patterned floor echoes that of the hall, but here the palette is muted, and the filmy grays of the walls and floor combine to produce the illusion of a misty atmosphere.

workable

The scale and classic geometry of a neutrally colored central
space are accentuated by the vibrant palette of surrounding rooms.

primaries

TALL WINDOWS WELCOME light into the perfectly proportioned main room of a converted nineteenth-century schoolhouse, the home of designer Birch Coffey. The walls of the large schoolroom are painted a yellowish parchment color to reflect the warmth of the sunlight and the honey tones of the pine floors. By painting this room in a neutral color the architecture can be experienced more fully and more attention paid to the volume of space itself than if bright planes of color had been chosen.

To further emphasize the exceptionally good bones of the main room—the symmetry of the square shape, the high ceiling and elegantly proportioned tall windows—all the trim is painted a stark, pure white. Even the chair-rail-height wainscoting is white, providing a visual link to the white window trim and the entire outlined structure of the room, drawing the eye upward and increasing the sensation of height.

Surrounding the large square central room is a procession of smaller, quirkily shaped rooms, each colored in a more definitive hue. The small entrance foyer, for example, is brick red; adjoining it is a narrow, windowless hallway painted a deep, rich green; a small bedroom

White-painted trim in the living room (LEFT) accentuates the good bones of this soaring central space; neutral parchment-colored walls let the room's volume itself be the focus. A view into the red entrance hall (PREVIOUS PAGE) provides a glimpse of two more vibrantly colored rooms, linked to the central space by white trim.

Parchment walls, warm
wood furniture, a gold mirror
frame, and richly colored
upholstery echo the honey
tones of the pine floor
and emphasize the abundant
natural light in the living
room. Accents of bright
yellow act as more literal
suggestions of sunlight.
Alliums gracefully imitate
the curving lines of an
iron chandelier.

just off the hall is colored a warm chamois. These more
vibrant colorations give the secondary spaces more
interest, drawing attention away from their imperfect
proportions and instead accentuating their chromatic
differences. To link the darker smaller rooms to the
center room, the trim also is painted in the same shiny
white throughout.

The more intense coloration of the secondary rooms
—similar in hue—also provides a contrast to the lighter,
less intense neutral color of the primary room, visually
emphasizing the differences between the two spaces and
making the transition into the grandly proportioned big
room more dramatic. The stronger colors of the smaller
rooms also add vitality to the house as a whole; in fact,
these sophisticated versions of primary colors seem particularly appropriate in this rejuvenated schoolhouse.

In the bedroom (RIGHT), the warm tones of the orange-yellow pine floors are carried up onto the walls and windows with chamois-colored paint and bamboo shades. Paired with white trim, the shiny black paint of the beds and armoire allows the chamois walls to form a background middle value. LEFT: This corner is enlivened with an array of warm hues.

color fields

color as

In this series of rooms, intersecting painted surfaces create distinct color compositions and a sense of their own architecture.

architecture

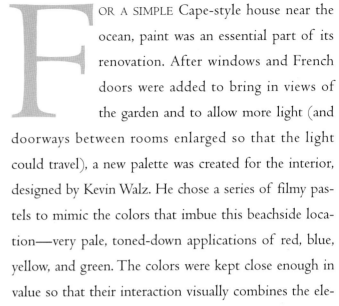

FOR A SIMPLE Cape-style house near the ocean, paint was an essential part of its renovation. After windows and French doors were added to bring in views of the garden and to allow more light (and doorways between rooms enlarged so that the light could travel), a new palette was created for the interior, designed by Kevin Walz. He chose a series of filmy pastels to mimic the colors that imbue this beachside location—very pale, toned-down applications of red, blue, yellow, and green. The colors were kept close enough in value so that their interaction visually combines the ele-

ments to form an overall soft, shimmering effect reminiscent of the atmospheric mist often found near the ocean.

To add interest to this house of low-ceilinged rooms with little detailing and standard narrow-board flooring, the decision was made to paint every surface, including the floors. The surfaces are painted in a mix of only slightly different colors; shifts are purposely subtle, as more dramatic contrasts would have drawn more attention to the architecture. Though a visitor experiences this house as full of color, the color has always been used with delicacy. Hues of a similar, muted intensity are artfully combined; no color is so strong that it stands out or is jarring.

A new sheet-metal wall studded with screwheads strikes through the middle of the house, forming one side of a central hall. Painted a creamy yellow, the wall works well as the center of a colorful house, with yel-

In the living room (ABOVE RIGHT), subtle value contrasts in the wall colors, compared to stronger contrasts with objects and furniture, heighten the illusion of filminess in the background. In the hall (OPPOSITE AND PREVIOUS PAGE), a studded metal wall is the sole grand architectural gesture; it is painted the warmest yellow and acts to anchor the colorful house.

low, the central hue of the spectrum, being neither too cold nor too warm. Stepping from the hall to the living room, the color of the walls remains a similar creamy shade but the floor changes from a cool blue to a paler shade of gray-blue. The contrast between walls and floors is lessened, and the room feels more enveloping.

From room to room, the changes in color, though subtle, are always noticeable. Each space is a distinct environment, carefully calculated with different colored walls and floors. The foundation of colored floors interacting with the colors of the walls and ceiling creates the feeling of moving through a series of colorful boxes. The intersection of color planes at the doorways is formed by hand-painted lines, becoming a part of the decoration of this house. Here, color actually is the architecture.

In this interior, every surface is painted, even the floors. Because a different palette was chosen for every room, each feels distinctive. The rooms appear like a series of colorful boxes, the transitions between them accentuated by the intersections of painted floors at each doorway.

planes

A long, narrow hallway is visually reshaped with a full spectrum
of interlocking paint colors, differentiating each architectural plane.

of color

FACED WITH THE UNINSPIRING vista of a very long, narrow hallway—a common decorating waterloo in urban apartments—a particularly painterly cure was devised for the home of art dealer Vivian Horan. The hall was divided into architectural planes, each painted in a different color. The interlocking color planes redefine the perception of the long hall, creating the feel of a series of different spaces.

The colors selected represent the full spectrum, which helps the passageway feel realized as a complete space. One side is painted in a cool, light palette; the other is painted in warm, darker colors. The contrast ensures that the eye always has complementary relief, and reaffirms that the

To redefine a long hallway (PREVIOUS PAGE), paint colors were selected to represent the full range of the spectrum (ABOVE). One side of the hall is painted with light, warm colors, the other with darker cool hues, the contrast giving the feel of an energetic transitional area. To visually link the two spaces, some of the paint colors relate to colors seen in the living room (OPPOSITE), the gray-green chairs and warm gold of the sisal carpet.

hallway is not a typical room setting. If the opposite walls were closer in color or value the hall would be experienced more as a room and have the feel of containment rather than motion and change. Some sections of color even turn the corner, giving that particular area a feeling of separateness from the other side of the hall; the paint wrapping the corner makes it almost appear as an actual object.

On both walls, colors in the center of the hall are the darkest. This adds to the feel of traveling through different spaces. One enters a light area, moves through a darker space, and reemerges into a light area. The lighter colors

also ease the transition to light-colored rooms that adjoin the hall at both ends. The creamy white of the ceiling, which extends down to the picture rail, serves to unify the disparate colors.

Some paint colors chosen for the hallway were selected to refer to other colors seen in the apartment, but they are purposely not overt matches. A pale golden paint in the hall can be linked to the honey-colored sisal in the living room; a deep green is an impressionistic echo of the furniture's dark gray-green upholstery.

The background here is balanced between warm and cool tones. Neutral white walls are paired with warm sisal and cool gray-green upholstery. This balanced background visually recedes, and objects, such as the intricately detailed black-lacquered side chair and a colorful collection of English Victorian glass bells, appear more pronounced.

complementary

The interaction of contrasting complementary colors makes minimally decorated rooms feel visually complete.

combinations

SOMETIMES A HOUSE can be furnished simply with the interaction of color. In a nineteenth-century farmhouse set in rolling horse country, minimal furnishings serve as structural elements in rooms that are actually decorated with color. Primary colors—different variations of yellows, reds, and blues—are used for the walls, trim, and floors, linked in complementary combinations. Interacting complementary colors cause the strength of each color to be emphasized. For example, in some rooms, apricot-colored walls make the adjacent blue trim appear grayer and more violet; peach walls make adjacent blues appear more green. Throughout the house, different combinations are used in concert; the exchanges of these primary colors enliven the space; the rooms feel fully realized, subtly complete.

Floors downstairs are a rich golden pine, polished to a high gloss and left uncovered; bare windows offer unencumbered views of blue sky. With this pairing of yellow and blue already in place, the same complementary palette is used for walls and trim. A visual framework is created from the strong golden tones of the floors and the deep blue of the trim, a vibrantly colored armature in which the dynamic interaction of color is contained. Peach walls echo the color of the floors; blue trim provides cool relief from the golden tones of the room while highlighting its warmth at the same time. Blue wrapped around the

The contrast of blue trim emphasizes the warmth of the orange pine floors and offers a cool respite. Softer variations of the floor hues are carried onto walls and create a similar exchange with the window trim. Apricot walls in the living room (PREVIOUS PAGE) **make the trim appear grayer; the dining room's peach walls push the blue trim toward green.**

The combinations of yellow with blue and red with green are often used complementary pairings in decorating. A wide range of both combinations is seen in the collection of objects on an old painted mantel (OPPOSITE) and in the bedroom (BELOW). Floorboards in the bedroom are salvaged barn siding with original paint; walls are painted yellow, a hue absent in the floors, that acts to complete the spectrum.

windows emphasizes the color of the sky and leads the eye out of the room, creating a feeling of space and an unlimited vista. The trim also visually brings the sky into the house, and this contrast strengthens the effect of the warm yellows of the floors and walls. The glow of the gold-leafed cornices that crown the windows in the living room mimics sunlight.

Upstairs, in the master bedroom, floors are made from old multicolored barn boards still covered with their original paint. Since yellow tones are missing in the floorboards, the bedroom walls are coated with a creamy yellow color. Throughout the house, little pattern is found; framed expanses of color are the only geometry. But pattern isn't necessary here—these spare interiors are furnished with colors, their lively exchange giving the rooms vibrance.

In a guest room (RIGHT), cool pale
walls provide a blue complement
to warm floors and adjacent yellow
bedroom, while white trim
softens the sense of framework in
the tranquil space. Throughout
the house, layers of original paint
on furniture and objects (ABOVE)
show primary oppositions
and complementary harmonies.

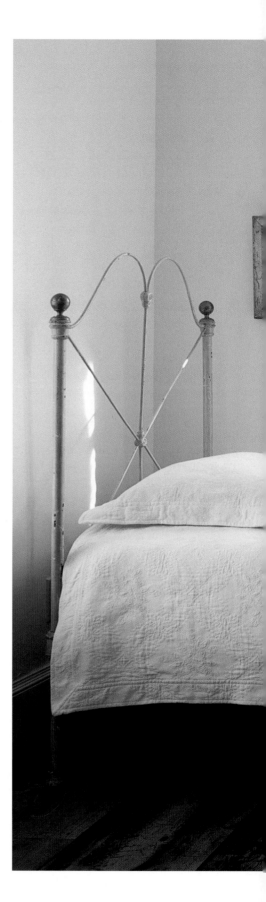

adding

Subtle gradations of color and texture create the illusion of
aged surfaces, adding a sense of history to newly plastered walls.

patina

AFTER THE COMPLETE renovation of a 1794 Connecticut farmhouse, new plaster walls suddenly looked a little *too* new. To integrate them more gracefully into their historic setting, thin coats of colored paint were washed over cream-colored walls. The resulting look, inspired by painting techniques seen in many early New England houses, gives more depth and a sense of permanence to the new construction and allows the new walls to coexist more naturally with the centuries-old detailing, such as the wide-board pine floors and the center-hall staircase, that still remains.

Interiors in the house are very spare—floors are left bare, window treatments are simple, furnishings minimal—so the colored walls are the only major decoration. Striking trim, painted in a wood-grain patterned glaze, frames each section of wall, making each plane of color appear almost as a painting—a perfectly framed composition. In varying degrees of yellow, red, and brown, the trim also adds warmth to all the rooms and helps to visually unify the different spaces; bare pine floors add a strong golden glow throughout.

Wall colors are rich golds and greens, subtly different but all sharing the same intensity. All of the color washes were created from flat latex paint, with a creamy base coat used first in all the rooms and then a topcoat of colored paint diluted with water (one part paint combined with four to eight parts water). White ceilings and the underlying base coat of the same cream

In the dining room (OPPOSITE **and** ABOVE)**, new plaster walls purposely left rough and the uneven green paint wash accentuate the play of light. The golden cast of the walls radiates from a warm, cream undercoat and is matched by the golden tones of the old pine floors.** PREVIOUS PAGE: Original details—the newel post and pine floorboards—exist comfortably with newly painted surfaces in the hall.

color on the walls give each of these vibrantly colored rooms equal weight so that no room upstages another. This is particularly important since furnishings are spare: Equality of color between the rooms helps keep the overall space in balance.

Color is vital, but texture is also important. Old paint was stripped from the woodwork in an intentionally uneven fashion, leaving vestiges of paint in crevices. New plaster was left rough. Not only do the resulting surfaces have an appealing patina of age, but the uneven surfaces beautifully accentuate the play of light and shadow. The coverage of the paint washes applied to the already irregular walls creates the feel of a natural surface developed over time. The color seems to be an authentic part of the history of the place, an integral component of the walls.

atmospheric
warmth

restrained

A subdued gray outline trim gives weight and substance
to the extravagant decorative flourishes of a rich yellow room.

pastels

INTENSE YELLOW WALLS accented with swaths of pastel pink draperies are an unexpected combination. But in an apartment designed by Baker & Sebesta, on Manhattan's Upper West Side, the addition of an architectural silhouette of cool gray trim proves to be the key to this surprisingly successful mix of colors.

Here, in a large living room ringed with tall windows, walls are painted a rich yellow and windows are dressed in voluminous pink silk taffeta draperies that flow from ceiling to floor. To create a structural outline to temper this extravagance of dramatic color, ceiling moldings and baseboards were painted a taupey gray. The gray outline adds weight and geometry to the room, and also acts as a counterbalance to the fanciful

Rich yellow walls make the living room seem always illuminated by the sun. The overall warmth of the room, created by the walls in combination with pink silk draperies, is carried onto the floor covered with honey-colored sisal. Gray moldings outline the space, adding an important geometry and counterbalance.

decorative accents, such as the taffeta draperies and a pink velvet-backed leopard throw. On the floor, honey-colored sisal echoes the warmth of the luminous yellow walls, and an over-size glass coffee table provides a touch of icy blue to complete the room's color spectrum.

To enter the living room, a visitor passes through the entrance foyer, painted a cool khaki. The foyer, visually linked to the living room with the same taupey gray trim, exists as a slightly cooler, more public environment and serves as a transition space to the more personal rooms beyond. The khaki color works as a neutral against the warm yellow of the living room, which is perceived as a subtle

source of light and thus tends to pull a visitor in. Light filtered through an amber beaded fixture warms the space, as do the golden tones of the parquet floor, the counterpart to the honey sisal of the living room.

The bedroom is a serene retreat, not as energized as the living room nor as cool as the foyer. A higher ceiling allowed the color to continue down the adjoining walls to the picture molding, making a visual cap. So, instead of colored walls below a white ceiling, the usual order was reversed and the color—a pale, mauvey pink—was used above, with white below. The room embodies a different dynamic than the active interchanges between strong colors found in the living room. Here, the softness of the colors and their closeness in value creates a contrast so subtle it evokes the feeling of an atmospheric mist.

The khaki entrance foyer (OPPOSITE) acts to anchor the fanciful flourishes of the adjacent living room while the same gray trim visually connects the spaces. In an unexpected reversal, the ceiling and wide sofitt of the bedroom (ABOVE) are painted in a pale pink hue while walls are painted white. In the living room (LEFT), creamy upholstery softens the array of decorative colors.

tempering

Carefully adjusted in temperature and intensity, apricot-colored
walls complement the warmth of burnished wood and antiques.

warmth

THE SPIRAL STAIRCASE in this 1810 Adam-style Colonial is the literal heart of the house. Rising four stories, the stairs strike dramatically through the center of the house and are crowned with a round leaded-glass skylight. The original mahogany stair treads and the floor of the center hall have deliberately been left uncovered so that light streaming through the skylight can bounce off the polished, rich surface of the wood. The atmosphere that is created travels through the core of the house, releasing warmth at every landing; a golden reflection illuminates the white ceiling.

Polished floors throughout the house are the original wide-board, honey-colored pine. Walls are painted

in various tints of a vibrant apricot, a carefully modulated color warm enough to comfortably blend with the brightness of the pine floors, but not so intense that it competes with the warmth of the furniture. The patina of the antique American furnishings and assortment of gilt objects, the iridescence of the silk draperies, even the luster of the American landscape paintings all emit a natural richness and glowing tone. The soft, light background allows these elements to be the real focus of the space.

Controlling both the temperature and intensity of a warm, decorative color like apricot is crucial. Here, the wall color acts to balance the bright, warm floors and creates an overall soft, warm background. A cooler wall color would have set up more of a contrast with the

floors, resulting in a less neutral, unified background, and thus giving less emphasis to the furniture and decorative objects. And if the walls were colored more intensely, upstaging the golds and greens of the draperies and upholstery, they would have made those colors look grayer in contrast.

The most casual room in the house, a small sitting room—far removed from the radiant central hall—is filled with comfortable, less formal furniture, where more playful colors feel appropriate. The room's trim is colored in a strong turquoise, which forms an outline against the white walls. The painted trim acts as a complement to the yellow-orange wood floor and is also of a similar intensity. The prominent architectural details of the house are still emphasized here, but in a more casual and exuberant way.

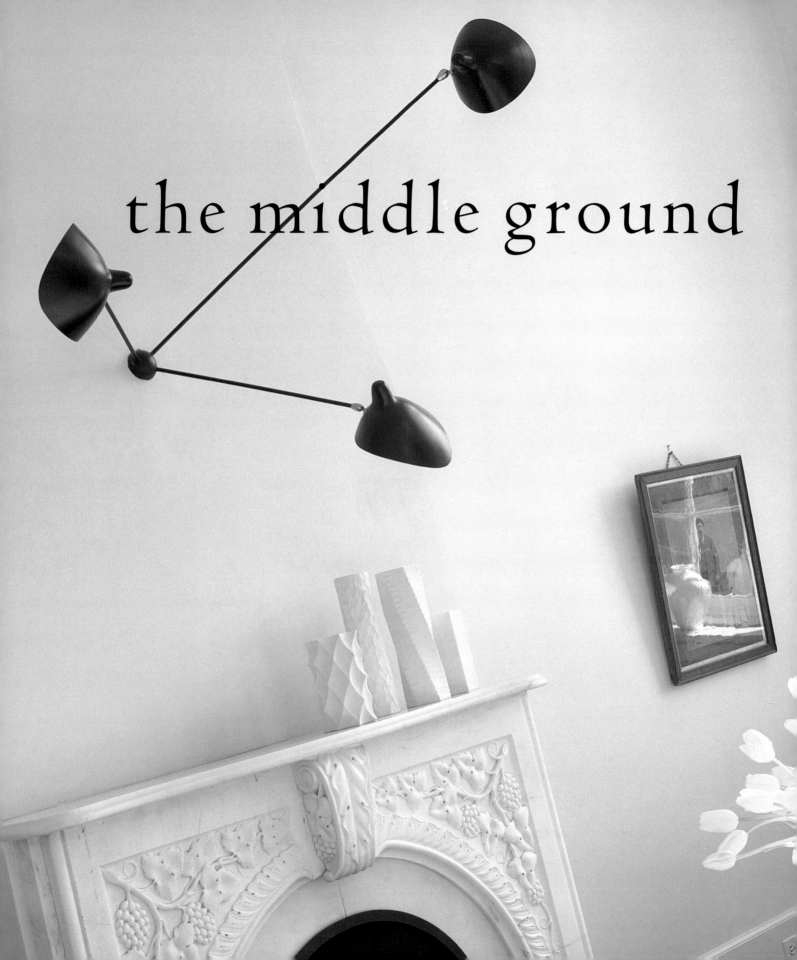

the middle ground

light and

The placement of light and dark neutrals is determined by the
architecture of the space and the amounts of natural light.

shadow

IN MANY MANHATTAN apartments, natural light is a precious commodity. But this duplex, in a turn-of-the-century building on a tree-lined street, proves an exception to the rule. The double-height living room has a tremendous asset: a long wall lined floor to ceiling with windows. Because the windows face south, the light streams in throughout the day. With this structure of light and geometry used as a focal point, the owners' first design decision was not difficult to make: The luminous living room would serve as the heart of the apartment. The dining room and entrance foyer, rooms with standard ceiling heights and little or no natural light, would play supporting roles.

Because the owners of this duplex, James Gager and Richard Ferretti, wanted the first floor to act as an antidote to the stresses and sounds of the outside world, they decided they wanted no jarring colors and no harsh whites. Instead, an overall palette of interplaying neutrals highlights the strong architectural bones of the space, with a hierarchy of color established among the rooms based on the amount of light they receive.

In the living room, walls are painted in the lightest neutral, a pale cream, to accentuate the abundance of light.

Both warm and cool pigments in the paint reflect the changing character of the light from golden morning to bluish dusk. Grounded by an ebony floor, this bright space seems to pop: The strong rectilinear shapes of the

The double-height living room (LEFT and PREVIOUS PAGE), flooded with natural light, is painted the palest neutral in the apartment. The color's warm and cool pigments reflect the changing character of the light throughout the day.

furniture (which also echo the grid of the windows) and the antenna-like armed lamps are sharply silhouetted. There is almost no pattern in the room, but remarkably, it never feels static—the play of light and shadow provides constant animation.

Every surface plays a role when determining a palette: walls, ceilings, trim, even floors. Here, floors are painted black throughout to visually anchor the space and give a feeling of continuity when moving from room to room. Not usually thought of as a neutral, black is actually the strongest neutral of all, able to impact powerfully on a room's color and clarity. For example, in the foyer, a room that receives almost no natural light, walls are painted a dark neutral, the color of a brown paper bag. And while the contrast of pale walls against dark flooring in the living room emphasizes the lightness of the space, in

The dining room (BELOW), **with lower ceilings and less light, is painted a warm beige, a medium neutral, that feels colorful compared to the light cream of the airy living room.**

The foyer (BELOW) receives no natural light; its deep neutral walls, with the ebony floor, create an enveloping space emphasizing the lightness of the living room. Upstairs (LEFT), creamy neutrals and a pale floor provide a background for colorful furnishings.

the foyer the deeply pigmented color contrasts very little with the dark floors, making the room feel small and enveloping. This atmospheric sense of a sheltered sanctuary enhances the dramatic feeling of airiness when a visitor looks into the soaring living room, as if viewing a stage from the wings.

A warm beige colors the walls in the dining room. Because French doors leading from the living room admit some natural light, the color is a medium neutral, about halfway in intensity between the colors of the foyer and living room. Compared to the pale, bright living room, the dining room and the foyer feel colorful; the level of color value adjusted to the lower level of light. And when one experiences all the rooms together, it is clear that each color subtly interacts with the others, so that one is drawn from room to room, and from dark to light.

a versatile

Pale neutral colors, shifting slightly from warm to cool tones, add variety to a classic black-and-white scheme.

background

A T FIRST GLANCE, the interiors in this small house near the ocean seem to be simply an elegant application of classic black and white, a favorite theme of the owner and designer, Jennifer Whitbeck. But looking carefully, the colors separate themselves into a varied collection of pale neutrals, with many shifts to cooler and warmer tones. Walls that appear white at first are actually gray; pale bleached pine floors are a light sand color. The layering of slightly different neutral hues in the space creates a livelier backdrop than would be created with a single color. Light, which streams in through the abundant windows and French doors, reacts in a different way with each slight variation in the colored surfaces. Even the neutral paint color on the walls incorporates a range of warm and cool pigments so that the wall color itself changes with the light. This balanced neutral color, with subtle shifts from warm to cool, modulates the background, adding variety to the contrast with objects in the foreground. The walls become a rich foil for the furnishings and decorative objects.

In the living room, walls painted in putty gray are slightly cooler than the warm blond of the wood floors but warmer than the cool "moon white" of the ceiling, which has a touch of blue; both the black and white elements of the room are clearly defined against this restrained color theme of warm and cool neutrals. The putty walls enable the white shapes of the

Putty gray walls in the living room (RIGHT) are cooler than the bleached floor but warmer than the cool moon-white ceiling creating an atmosphere behind the black and white furniture, upholstery, and objects. Painted white trim outlines architectural details (PREVIOUS PAGE).

trim and the furniture to act as silhouettes just as black elements do (like the piping on the chaises, black picture frames, and the boldly striped pillows).

Pattern also heightens the interplay of contrasts. The kitchen incorporates the same pale wood flooring as the other rooms, but the introduction of painted black diamonds causes the wood to appear as a different color than the floor in the rest of the house. The floor's interlocking blocks of sand and black fool the eye into seeing them as white and black, as in a classic black and white tiled floor.

The basic black and white armature created throughout this house becomes a framework, making any other color that is introduced a strong presence. The brilliant crimson of a wool throw or the yellow tones of a gold frame are noticeable gestures in this environment.

Subtle shifts from warm to cool tones seen along the wall (BELOW) allow for more contrast with the objects in front of it. The black and white acts to highlight any other color, such as the crimson throw (OPPOSITE), making it appear an even stronger accent.

The same blond wood
floor continues into the
kitchen (OPPOSITE),
where the addition of
painted black diamonds
makes it appear as
a classic black-and-white
floor. Its pattern
heightens the interplay
of contrasts, which appear
more subtly elsewhere,
as in the hall (LEFT).

dissolving

One light, warm neutral acts to unify a group of undefined spaces, while deeper values delineate more traditional rooms.

boundaries

FTENTIMES, CHOOSING wall colors for a contemporary space is a particular challenge. In these less traditional floor plans, rooms tend to flow into one another, without doors or other architectural changes to delineate the spaces. Thus, one wall color must be selected that will work equally well in each area.

In a New York City penthouse, interior designer DeDe Allen encountered low-ceilinged rooms with little architectural detailing that opened into each other, cre-

ating a large central space. She decided not to impose definition between the areas with different wall colors. Instead, a single creamy yellow wall color was chosen to completely dissolve the boundaries. The warm pale yellow walls give the illusion of actually emitting light and maximize the luminous effects of the natural light that enters the apartment. Yellow also helps to counteract the coldness of the shadows cast by deep recessed windows; a cooler neutral would have emphasized their violet tinge.

In areas that are more architecturally separated from the central space, such as the library, which has a clearly defined entrance outlined with molding, the wall color shifts to a soft mossy green, which serves to heighten the impact of the transition into a new room. Green is also used on the staircase that leads from the main living area of the apartment to the second floor. Its dramatic swirl of deep green treads adds contrast, highlighting

Light neutral walls and ceiling paired with pale neutral floors (BELOW) keep the focus on the Mark Rothko painting and the exuberantly patterned needlepoint rug. The central staircase (OPPOSITE) is a main focal point of the apartment; deep green treads emphasize its dramatic curving shape, the dark hue adding the sensation of traveling a greater distance.

More architecturally defined
areas such as the study (RIGHT)
are painted in deep values and
more colorful hues, the contrast
setting them off from the
free-flowing central space. The
interplay of red, green, and
gold throughout the apartment is
also seen here. The series of
pastels are by Francesco Clemente.

In the dining room (BELOW),
the ceiling is covered not
with paint, but with silver
tea paper. The soft,
reflective surface visually
softens the edges of the low
ceiling and provides a
shimmering setting for the
Fortuny hanging lamp.
The complementary blue of
the velvet-covered chair
in the bedroom (OPPOSITE)
makes the walls seem
more yellow.

its importance as an architectural element and empha-sizing the dynamic curve of the stairs.

The Rothko painting can provide a key to the palette. The complementary red and green colorfields of the canvas are held in place by a framework of orangey gold —an artful illustration of the fact that metallic gold is a scintillating play between red and green polarities. A version of this dynamic can be experienced in the sur-rounding environment. Green areas ring a core of yellow space; red is seen in the patterned Deco-inspired carpet, in the artwork on the walls, and most emphatically in the burgundy upholstery of the library's armchairs.

In the dining room, silver tea paper was used to make the low ceiling an asset rather than a liability. Its rich reflective surface would be noticed less and its impact diminished if the ceilings were higher.

highlighting

Balanced warm and cool neutrals provide a subtle framework
for the brilliant hues and strong shapes of a folk-art collection.

a collection

SUCCESSFULLY INTEGRATING collections into an interior can be a very delicate balancing act. In Linda Cheverton and Walter Wick's 1820 Connecticut house, a complementary environment has been created to highlight objects both ordinary and precious.

Since their collection of folk art is constantly changing and because the pieces themselves are often vibrantly colored, the couple wanted to compose an atmosphere that would enhance the art but not compete with it. Original wainscoting and moldings throughout the house provided a structural framework, and were colored to represent a careful balance of values. Painted in a tight range of cream, putty, and gray, the backgrounds blend and emphasize the outlines of the objects in the foreground, allowing them to stand out clearly.

An interplay of warm and cool tones ensures that although the walls and floors are technically neutrals, there is enough contrast to create visual interest. Therefore, the putty of the wainscoting in the entrance foyer and dining room is warmer than the white walls but slightly cooler than the yellow pine floors. The colors are present in equal amounts and are of similar inten-

In the kitchen, buttermilk-colored trim complements blues in a collection of objects (OPPOSITE) and echoes the colors of the 1920s English pottery by Susie Cooper. In the dining room (RIGHT), Pennsylvania painted chairs and a Mexican religious figure stand out in bold relief against a carefully calibrated backdrop of warm and cool neutral colors.

sity, so that the temperature remains balanced; however, the balance is adjusted from room to room so that slightly different atmospheres are created.

In the foyer and the living room, cool white walls are combined with the yellow of bare pine floors. In the dining room, since the floorboards are painted in a putty color, a sisal rug adds honey-colored warmth, as does the wood tabletop. Artwork and furniture appear distinct and jewel-like against this neutral backdrop, making the coloration of the rooms complete. Painted artworks bring miniature vignettes of full-spectrum color to a neutral setting.

In the living room, the white walls are paired with cream-painted trim, a barely perceptible difference in color. This creates a casual framework, identifying the sunny room as a place of relaxation.

The diminished contrast between walls and trim in the living room (ABOVE), lessens the sense of framework for display, making the room feel relaxed and inviting. The taupe-gray trim in the foyer (RIGHT) mediates between the warmth of the orange pine floors and the cool putty walls, while vivid painted objects such as the nineteenth-century shop figure match the floor in intensity. OPPOSITE: In this setting, a salvaged cupboard door becomes another art object.

interacting

A collection of varied hues is determined by the setting and function
of each room, while a single trim color acts as a unifying device.

hues

A SIMPLE ACKNOWLEDGMENT of the influence of a few key variables decided the palette of this early-nineteenth-century Manhattan town house. In the living room, for example, the pale yellow of the wall color was decided by an inherited Oriental rug: Since the rug's palette was composed mainly of reds and blues, yellow was needed to round out the spectrum. Even the view outside the window was considered—the yellow paint has undertones of green so that it will complement the trees. The gilt detailing and gold upholstery of the furniture add to the golden cast of the room, and since the combination of red and green creates gold, so do the red tones of the unfinished pine floor mixed with the greenish cast of the walls. To emphasize the perfect cubic proportions of

A paled-down yellow used on the walls and ceiling of the living room (OPPOSITE) keeps the perimeter soft, making the room seem bigger and emphasizing its cubic proportions. Looking out of the living room (LEFT), the warmth of the yellow walls is more pronounced against the cool white of the hall. In the dining room (PREVIOUS PAGE), painted deep-green walls are warmed by the addition of red and yellow pigments, and a yellow ceiling.

the room, the ceiling was painted the same color as the walls, blanketing the room in a subdued golden khaki light. With early-morning sun, the barrier between inside and out seems to almost disappear.

Looking from this luminous space to the hallway, the contrast between the rich yellow of the living room and the pale gray in the hall is highlighted. One space is contemplative, a room meant to be lingered in; the other is a room to be moved through. The yellow walls and raw wood floors warm the living room; the gray walls and reflective, high-gloss floors cool the hall.

In the dining room, the color shifts even more dramatically. In this streetside room, deep green walls mark a definitive barrier against the noise. In addition to the high-contrast wall color, window shutters were added to physically help shut out the outside. Because

The hallway's cool gray-white walls and reflective floor (OPPOSITE) are more appropriate for a space to pass through, not to linger in. Cream trim appears more yellow here in contrast to the walls, and acts as a complement to the pale violet ceiling. Old shutters in the bedroom (RIGHT) create an engaging play of light and shadow, drawing the eye to the windows.

they are the same raw wood as the floors, they stand out starkly against the green of the walls. Shutters in the living room are painted the same color as the rest of the trim to visually blur the boundary between the room and the view. The choice of green for the dining room is an unusual one since the cool blue element of the color does not especially enhance food. To modify the blue's coolness, the paint contains a careful counterbalance of red and yellow pigments, and the ceiling, painted a strong yellow, makes the room seem more golden than blue.

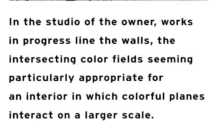

In the studio of the owner, works in progress line the walls, the intersecting color fields seeming particularly appropriate for an interior in which colorful planes interact on a larger scale.

The trim color, a rich cream, is the same throughout, serving to unify the spaces. With only one color, there is never a jarring effect of different trims meeting at every doorway. Though it is a constant, the color adjusts itself in different rooms. In the living room, the moldings blend easily with the pale yellow of the walls, making the edges of the room disappear and the space feel expansive; in the hall, the trim looks more yellow and makes the cool white walls appear more violet. In the deep green dining room, the pale baseboards and door frames seem whiter in contrast to the wall color, emphasizing the enveloping, atmospheric feel of the darker palette. This constant interplay of colors rubbing up against each other, challenging the supremacy of the other, makes the total space a subtly nuanced treat for the eye.

cool

The eye is naturally drawn to the intense warmth
of one room in the heart of a very cool space.

neutrals

IN THIS NEW YORK PENTHOUSE, a palette of grayed-off greens and khakis seems to meld with outside views of similar neutrals seen in the skyline and distant landscape. Ceilings are not high in the apartment, and rooms open onto each other with little defining architectural detail. An ebony-stained floor flowing throughout the space acts as a unifying factor and leads the eye away from the low ceilings by visually anchoring the rooms. Since the difference in value between the walls and dark floors is more pronounced than between walls and ceiling, the eye is naturally drawn downward to the area of greatest contrast. The dark floor also helps the medium-value walls to remain neutral and seem less dark. Placed

Terra-cotta and burgundy tones in the study (PREVIOUS PAGE) seem richer in contrast to the complementary khaki greens in the surrounding rooms (ABOVE). Relative to the other colors, the study's terra-cotta ceiling (OPPOSITE) is the warmest color of the palette. The burgundy patterned carpet adds spark to the room's deeper atmosphere.

with lighter floors, these walls would have seemed more "colorful." In other areas, trim has the opposite effect, making green walls appear more green and less neutral. Gray painted trim in the living and dining rooms and upholstered furniture in varying tones of gray also act to soften the contrasts and to keep the perimeter hues neutral.

Red accents are used to great effect in this overall gray-green palette—from the red upholstery in the living room to the warm red tones of the highly polished furniture in the dining room. In neutral spaces, our attention is naturally drawn to objects, and the red objects here exploit their comple-

Walls are green enough to set off the red chaise (LEFT) without becoming gray and cold in contrast. In the kitchen (BELOW), a green-painted floor is dark enough so that it remains visually linked to ebony floors in other rooms.

mentary association to create focus while at the same time reflecting essential warmth.

The most dramatic illustration of the effect of this complementary contrast of red and green is seen in the center of the apartment, in the relationship between the wood-paneled study and the surrounding rooms. The paneling is a deep brownish red, the ceiling is papered in a rich terra-cotta, even the carpet has deep red tones. The eye is drawn through the apartment to the enveloping warmth of this room; it acts as the intensely warm heart of a very cool space.

Accents of white make
deep-neutral wall colors
seem more saturated.
In the bathroom (ABOVE)
white trim makes green
walls appear deeper green,
while even the gray walls
of a guest bedroom
seem stronger in contrast
to white linens (RIGHT).

colors of

Strong colors can appear almost as neutrals in an interior carefully tied to its surroundings.

the landscape

COLORS DRAWN FROM the surrounding landscape of forest and a shade garden have been carefully incorporated into the interior of this early-nineteenth-century home in Connecticut. The atmospheres of the inside and outside are so perfectly reflected that the rooms feel like a continuation of the outdoors. Stepping stones from the garden lead up to the front door. The brownish red color of the garden shed appears on the walls of the living room. The gray seen in the stones and in the natural brush fence is found in the gray doors and window trim of the studio.

Many of the interior paint colors are a reflection of outside materials—stone, wood, iron, straw—and thus exist as neutrals. These colors are of the same intensity as their outdoor counterparts, so there is not a wide-ranging palette but a scrupulously restricted one. The paint in the interiors is used sparingly but to maximum effect: The bluish gray in the studio is not spread over the walls, but contained on the trim; a rusty red-colored wall in the sitting room adjoins a wall of fieldstone and unfinished wood. Because the surfaces to be painted were deliberately left rough, the variations in texture make the paint colors feel as if they actually come from a natural material.

Every detail inside and out fits into this natural palette: Garden ornaments are found objects from the woods, like the uprooted tree stump nestled in ferns. The unique environment created here, restrained in tone, is tied inextricably to its natural surroundings.

PREVIOUS PAGE and RIGHT: Garden stepping stones lead directly into the house and relate to the hearth stones. The brick red of the shed is echoed in the living room wall color; a neatly stacked woodpile corresponds to the basket of brown paper kindling.

LEFT: The weathered brush fence built by the owner conforms to the natural forms in the garden and repeats colors used indoors. In this house there is hardly any perception of boundaries between inside and out.

The barn is used as a studio by
the owners, an artist and a photog-
rapher. The colors are from
natural materials: weathered wood
beams and floors, wicker, steel,
linen and canvas, all found in the
furnishings and architecture of
their home. The sole paint color, a
bluish gray used on the trim, is
a reference to the gray brush fence.

color as
structure

a gestural

The warm wood and exuberant form of architectural details are accentuated in contrast to cool painted surfaces.

framework

THE ARCHITECTURE of an interior can make such a strong statement that adding obvious color would only dilute its effect. In this 1896 Manhattan town house, original detailing creates an architectural armature so intriguing that walls are deliberately left neutral. Exuberant moldings and trim reflect a hodgepodge style of architecture popular at the time, dubbed Elizabethan Renaissance Revival, where a variety of decorative elements were available ready-made.

The contrast between dark and light—between the reddish mahogany of the trim around the doors and windows and the flat planes of the pale walls—creates the illusion of depth, adding a sense of movement and life to the space. The warmth of the wood also gives the trim added strength in relation to the cool walls, visually forcing them to recede. Grand architectural shapes like the arch over the fireplace and the soaring window frames appear even more monumental. The highlighted architectural detailing becomes a graphic element, similar to the chiaroscuro of a pen-and-ink drawing or a black-and-white photograph. Color on the walls would have reduced the energetic byplay between dark warmth and cool neutral.

The color of the ceiling cornices is close to the wall colors, but the relationship between the two changes slightly from room to room. In the living room (PREVIOUS PAGE), the cornice color contrasts more with the walls, providing a visual balance to the mahogany detailing. Since there is less wood trim in the library (OPPOSITE), the contrast between wall and ceiling is downplayed.

Though painted ceiling cornices seem similar in color to the walls, the slightly darker color of the moldings is significant. In the living room, a light wall color is paired with a smoky cornice, which adds emphasis to the intricate dentil work; the contrasting paint colors help the room keep its balance against the strong lines of the mahogany detailing. In the library, with less dark wood, the wall color is slightly deeper, and so the contrast between walls and ceiling cornice is lessened.

Furnishings continue the palette; pale painted floors and putty-colored linen upholstery echo the walls' cool neutrals. Warm wooden pieces like the lacquered chestnut tansu chest and a Venezuelan folk art tapir relate to the mahogany trim. In this neutral framework, designed by Celeste Cooper, the focus is on the diverse collection of objects and their materials.

strong

Cream walls and mahogany trim create a play of light
and dark, leading the eye through a richly detailed space.

details

RICHLY POLISHED mahogany flows throughout this New York City apartment, emphasizing the architectural outlines of the space. Windows, doorways, and ceilings are all delineated by the dark trim, some walls paneled completely in the rich wood. To accentuate and act as balance to the strong personality of the wood, all the walls and ceilings are painted a warm creamy white. This color acts as a crisp foil for the reddish brown of the wood but is balanced to contain enough red and yellow pigments to not appear cold by comparison. A cooler white would be too contrasting, pushed to a bluish cast by the millwork's depth and warmth.

The contrast between light walls and dark trim brings interest and energy to the apartment—the interaction

Cream paint used throughout is warm enough to remain neutral against the rich mahogany trim. The contrast of light and dark at the perimeter captures the attention of the viewer, and as the eye actively follows the path of the trim, it almost seems to furnish the space.

between the two colors at the perimeter of the spaces leads the eye from room to room as it follows the path of the mahogany. To a visitor moving through the space, vistas seen through doorways are outlined in wood, and framed views, much like paintings, are created.

The single color of the interiors, designed by Mariette Himes Gomez, allows the exquisitely crafted detailing to stand as the strongest decorative element in the space. Not only walls, but the pale sisal on the floor and the light taupes of the upholstered furniture contribute to the cream palette, with wood accent pieces subtly reinforcing the importance of the mahogany trim. The contrast of the cream interiors against the dark trim makes the wood stand out more clearly as a material; the carefully wrought detail of the mahogany is more pronounced in these white rooms, whereas in a room painted red, the delineation of the wood trim would have been obscured. The single-color palette also draws attention to the textures of the creamy elements: the soft velvet of the taupe upholstery, the smooth cottons and linens of the white bedding, the nubby wool of sisal carpeting. Only with this restricted palette could these subtleties be brought to life with such force.

The cream palette is continued in the paled tones of velvet and linen upholstery and sisal carpeting, allowing the dark wood to be the most prominent element. The contrast also helps to accentuate the wood as a material, since a more colorful hue would draw attention away from it.

In the bedroom (LEFT),
beams are painted in the
same cream as the ceiling
itself, creating a visual
softening between the two
planes. The single-color
palette draws attention to
the varied textures—of
upholstery fabrics and bed-
linens in the bedroom
and in hand-painted mosaic
tiles in the bathroom
(ABOVE). In the dressing
room (RIGHT), trim becomes
a picture frame of the
reflection in the mirror.

In a home that combines both old buildings and new construction,
the color of painted trim changes in response to its setting.

THE STRUCTURAL BEAMS and original wood trim in this eighteenth-century home were too important to be obscured. Now they stand as the most prominent elements of the architecture. The home is actually a seamless compound, formed from a 1780 tobacco barn and an eighteenth-century cottage, linked with a newly constructed space that echoes the feel of the ancestral buildings.

The strong structural elements in the original buildings are highlighted by white unpainted plaster ceilings and walls; only windows, doors, and their surrounding trim are painted with color, though the deep color choices are strong enough to make these components feel structural as well. In the old barn/living room, the trim is painted

In the living room, originally a tobacco barn, the deep green paint used on the trim and bookcases seems substantial and structural, appropriate for the 18th-century building. The paintings are by owner John Funt. In the kitchen (ABOVE), a wall paneled with old painted doors adds the impression of age to new construction.

a dark green; in the cottage/bedroom it is a deep blue. These dark, easily recognizable hues appear structural compared to decorative colors like ephemeral pinks or mauves; they seem to be consistent with the feeling of supporting weight and more appropriate for these bold buildings. Even the intense green guestroom trim relates to the "natural" color ranges of the old structures, but in a more decorative way. It also introduces the perception of trim as furniture as well as structure.

In the new section of the house, painted trim provides a sense of support as well. Since the new space lacks the weighty patina of age inherent in the older buildings, the trim color, a taupey beige, is not as strong;

In the new section, trim painted
a taupey beige contrasts less with
white walls and appears less
overtly structural than does the
darker trim in the old parts
of the house. Uneven plaster walls
and rough-hewn stone hearths
crafted by local artisan Mark
Mendel are echoes of old buildings.

this lighter and more neutral color plays down the effect of the structural outline system, although not so completely that it is obliterated. The trim color here relates to the old wooden beams but does not compete with them—it has been given a lighter value so that the contrast with the white plaster walls is lessened and it simply diminishes the impact a bit.

The trim's taupey beige also has a grayish cast, which links it to the addition's stone hearths and weathered wood floors, grounding the color to the space. Designer John Funt selected a low-key neutral palette to let this area exist comfortably as a transition between the more dramatic parts of his house. It is evocative of the original buildings but does not merely try to imitate.

In an 18th-century cottage that now serves as a bedroom/sitting room (RIGHT), white plaster walls contrast with dark blue trim, accentuating the sense of strong structure. In a guest bedroom (ABOVE), trim is painted in a vivid green reminiscent of a green used in 18th-century interiors.

a bold

Intense color makes handcarved trim a bold decorative
gesture, while lighter and darker values temper its impact.

outline

T O CELEBRATE the exuberant profusion of carved-wood trim in his Connecticut home, architect Frank Garretson chose an unexpectedly vibrant color: a bold Prussian blue. The strong color doesn't seem such a surprising choice when, on closer inspection, the hand-carved trim is revealed to be a quixotic mix of architectural styles culled from the eighteenth and nineteenth centuries. And in fact, the trim, with its echoes of Georgian and Federal elements, embellishes a newly constructed house.

The intense color calls attention to the extensiveness of this handcrafted detailing, making it an even more powerful decorative element of the interior. Though some early American houses contained strong colors, the owner was not interested in making a literal translation; rather, he simply enjoyed the unusual juxtaposition of vibrantly colored trim against white plaster walls. A translucent glaze applied over the blue paint of the trim adds texture and nuance; the resulting slight variations in the surface temper the otherwise flat, uniform quality of the intense color.

To complement the blue, raw, unfinished pine floors add a broad expanse of yellow and provide the interest of contrasting texture: the unfinished matte quality of the floors playing against the shiny surface of the

In the upstairs hall, pine trim is painted with a golden wood-grain glaze; the yellow tones act as complement and relief to the blue trim downstairs. PREVIOUS PAGE: A broad expanse of hand-planed white pine flooring, left unfinished and uncovered, is a powerful complement to the vibrant blue glaze of the trim.

The bold color of the trim is a mix of Prussian and cerulean blues created by local artist Roz Leach; a coat of striated glaze adds textural nuance and tempers its intensity. Light-colored upholstery on dark furniture (LEFT) allows the blue trim to be perceived as a medium value. A massive Italian urn (OPPOSITE) is a yellow focus for the surrounding blue bands.

painted trim. Upstairs, the hallway acts to both complement and relieve the blue; it is a primarily yellow space, with golden pine floors.

Interestingly, the furnishings of the house affect the way that the intense blue is perceived. The strongly contrasting elements in the furniture—dark frames paired with light upholstery—allow the trim to be perceived as having a medium value. Despite its strength, the trim still seems part of the background, against which the furniture is outlined.

benefits of simplicity

the richness

The use of a single rich color, a vibrant red, gives impact
to a raw space and makes its surfaces feel more substantial.

of red

IN AN URBAN LOFT, a decision to paint all the walls one color isn't surprising. Usually, however, that color choice is white. But this apartment, painted a deep garnet red, proves that an expanse of even a strong color doesn't have to be overwhelming. To be sure, red walls are a bold gesture, but it is surprising how easily the eye becomes accustomed to it. With one color used everywhere, even this emphatic red actually acts more like a neutral—the color's impact diminishes. The longer you are surrounded by it, the more gray and less intense the red appears.

This is not to say that vibrant red walls have no effect on the loft's environment. Though the color may be modulated by its sheer expanse, the brilliant red still adds a bounty of warmth and energy to the space. One reason the red's impact remains vital is its placement between white floors and white ceilings. Because it is bracketed by its most extreme contrasting noncolor (white is an even stronger contrast than black, the other noncolor) the impact of the walls is heightened. White objects placed judiciously throughout—the column-base table, the sculpture, and a grid of white-framed and white-matted etchings—also strengthen the effect.

To stand up to the dynamic wall color, other elements in the space must be equally strong. Chairs dressed with vibrant ultramarine velvet and a wall draped in blue-gray flannel provide complementary color. Furnishings have been kept simple; distracting clutter is at a minimum. The shapes of the upholstered sofa and settees, designed by the owner, Philip Hohenlohe, are cleanly sculptural; their mohair-velvet upholstery was the inspiration for the garnet walls. Against the starkness of the raw space and straightforward objects, the lavish spill of red walls provides a welcome richness, making the surfaces seem more substantial and adding luxury to a space unadorned with architectural detailing.

ABOVE, LEFT: Painted walls seem to have almost as much depth and texture as a wall draped in gray flannel. OPPOSITE: Deeply recessed windows are painted white to reflect sunlight. This trim also accentuates the windows' shape, and makes them appear more as objects, prominent against the red background.

variations

A streamlined palette provides a versatile background
for an interplay of warm and cool contrasts.

of green

168

OR A NEW YORK APARTMENT that over-
looks the treetops of Central Park, the
choice of a green interior seemed completely natural. On a spring or summer
day, looking outside on the canopy of
leaves, one can distinguish surprisingly unlimited variations of this color—from brilliant yellow-greens to
deepest blue-greens. This wide spectrum of greens is
mimicked in the apartment's interior, a graceful reflection of what lies outside.

The small residence, in a postwar building, had little
original architectural character, so
designer Mary Moore simply built it
in, adding columns, chair rails, crown
molding, and a grid of bookshelves.
Since the different rooms flow into
each other, green was used to unify the
space, helping to ease the transitions
between them. So that the single-color
palette did not become relentless,
many different hues were used. Green
is a particularly good color choice
because it has both warm (yellow) and
cool (blue) aspects, and can easily
change temperature with the addition
of yellow or blue pigments. It also
appears warmer in a space containing
blue accents and cooler when combined with reds or yellows.

**In the foyer (ABOVE) the deeper
green door emphasizes the
entrance. In the living room
(RIGHT), painted a cool lime-yellow,
the rich golds of the gilt mirror and
painted screen add warmth.
Contrasting with these warm notes
are a cooler bluish green carpet
and upholstered furniture.**

The entrance foyer is a grayish green, with recessed
lighting and the golden tones of the inlaid floor, adding
just enough warmth to feel inviting. The deep green of
the front door anchors the space, and gives the entrance

Walls in the the bedroom
(LEFT) and library (RIGHT)
are light khaki green.
Reds and yellows seen in
the burnished wood of
the floors and furniture
further warm these spaces,
making them seem
enveloping and intimate.

impact. The living room is painted the palest lime yellow. A sky blue ceiling and the blues and blue-greens of the upholstered furniture and rug add cool notes while the polished wood floors and the gold tones of the mirror and folding screen add warmth. This constant interplay between warm and cool generates activity and adds interest to the room, the largest and the most public space.

The smaller, more private rooms are set off by slightly darker colors. Walls in the library are a light khaki green, so that the transition from the living room's pale green walls is seamless but there is enough added warmth to make the room feel intimate and enveloping. The reds and yellows of the wood floors and furniture plus bright accents of books become allies of the yellow side of green and empha-size the warmth of this space. The bedroom is painted in the same khaki, but the deeper reds of the room—burnished woods and accents of burgundy in the rug and fabrics—heighten the sense of sanctuary.

The changes between warm and cool greens seen as one walks through the apartment seem familiar—they are the variations one would encounter walking through a forest, and they illustrate the strengths of this verdant palette.

paper-bag

In an interior defined by a range of natural materials, painted walls appear to be covered with brown craft paper.

brown

THOUGH THE WOOD detailing in this 1914 Long Island house near the ocean is particularly striking—burnished mahogany doors are original, as are the dark-stained floors in every room—it wasn't the only element considered when the palette for the interior was chosen. The strong graphic lines of the owner's collection of framed photographs and the distinctive shapes of his British colonial furniture were also integral components and had just as much influence on the decisions.

Since the wood surfaces are perceived both as a color (dark brown) and as a material, the decision was made to paint the walls in a color that suggests another "material": a brown the color of a paper bag. This paper-bag color appears integral to the surfaces; it doesn't just cover the walls, it seems to be *in* the walls. The eye identifies the color as a material because of its cultural association with the rough craft paper of a grocery bag.

Terra-cotta red is a similar type of color; we not only see a rusty red, but identify it with clay or brick.

The paper-bag brown walls also work well because they match the abundant wood in warmth and provide a rich foil for furnishings present in a restricted palette of neutrals. With the addition of white trim, a series of contrasting frameworks is formed: light areas surrounded with dark, and dark areas with light. White trim throughout the house borders darker walls, doors, and floors; dark wood frames surround the white-matted photographs that line the walls. Even furnishings

Throughout the house, a series of dark and light frameworks can be seen, from the white trim that delineates the brown walls to the dark wood frames of the Edward S. Curtis photographs. PREVIOUS PAGE: In another play of light and dark, sheer muslin slipcovers silhouette the carved backs of dining room chairs.

The blue bathroom (LEFT)
is a pleasing anomaly
in this brown-toned house,
seeming to echo the
archetypal pairing of brown
earth and blue sky. In
the bedroom (OPPOSITE),
textural furnishings are
in a tight range of colors
that seem to be indigenous
to their materials; the
layering of linen, parch-
ment, and suede in similar
hues recalls palettes
seen in nature, limited yet
infinitely varied.

seem to be arranged as tight compositions and appear almost as still lifes—with backgrounds formed by the painted wall, the white molding acting as a frame.

The house, owned by lighting designer Greg Yale, is expressed in a very tight range of colors and materials. Rooms are filled with teak, mahogany, and leather; fabrics are almost exclusively unbleached muslin and linen; carpeting is rough sisal. With hardly a color present that does not come from the natural material itself, walls painted in paper-bag brown seem natural too. The limited palette—parchment to eggnog, wheat to umber—layered in a variety of textures, provokes the same feeling as a landscape: pleasing in its sameness, made beautiful by the slight changes in color and texture. The effectiveness of such a simple palette is often revealed to us when we look at nature.

a cream

Close-range pale neutrals surrounded by rich creamy walls evoke a sense of tranquillity.

palette

A SINGLE NOTE, a neutral paint the color of rich Devonshire cream, unifies the subtle mix of natural materials in this interior and also acts as a foil for the owners' collection of graphically shaped modern furniture and the graceful forms of Japanese objects.

Furnishings are in a palette of pale neutrals: Light-colored maple furniture with woven raffia and linen upholstery sits on floors of stone and bleached wood. The cream wall paint, used throughout, ensures little interruption in the overall tone of the space and evokes the serenity we associate with traditional Japanese interior architecture. This creamy color acts as a connecting neutral, mediating between the other colors present in the space—between the warmth of the wool sisal and

Black is used to visually contain and emphasize filmy neutrals and as a framing device to accentuate the shapes of furniture and objects. Wool sisal carpet bordered in black is a reference to tatami mats (PREVIOUS PAGE). The black outline of an antique chest is echoed in the grid of the dark wood railing (OPPOSITE and RIGHT). A full spectrum of pigments in the cream walls lets them interact with both warm and cool components, such as the cool gray painting and warm maple furniture.

Magritte   *South Bank Centre*

NOLDE *The Painter's Prints*

OUT OF THE FIRE

THE ART OF JAPANESE PRINTS   RICHARD ILLING

VAN GOGH

the blond wood furniture and the cooler cast of the pale wood floors and the gray linen upholstery of the chaise. Because the paint combines both warm and cool polarities from the full spectrum of pigments that it contains, it is able to both complement and contrast with each of the slightly different color temperatures seen against it. In the spare interior, the variations present in this painted background highlight the strong linear and geometric shapes of the furniture and cause objects to appear almost as sculptures.

There are new takes on Japanese motifs in this space, designed by Celeste Cooper: The wool sisal carpet is bound with black cotton tape to echo the look of a tatami mat; window "screens" are made of a fine fishnet. Light filtered through this filmy fabric creates a misty atmosphere, a feeling mimicked by the delicate interaction between all the close-range colors present.

In an unexpected way, there is a broad palette represented, with a perfectly balanced neutral in the middle and white and black at either end. No overt colors are used, but the subtle nuances of the natural textures and the slight variations in tone from warm to cool make the interiors feel spectrally complete. The black edges of things, while they take up less surface area, are no less important than the paler neutral fields. These borders—seen in the banded carpet, the railing, the edge of the painting, the lines of the taped chairs—form an armature that contains the filmy neutrals. Black is an especially effective framing device here, not only because of its darkness, but because of its neutrality.

The combination of black, white, and balanced neutrals creates a surprisingly broad palette. Variations in natural textures and the play of warm and cool tones make the environment feel spectrally complete. Lengths of fishnet hung at the windows diffuse sunlight, creating an atmosphere in which the borders of the room feel indistinct.

spectrum of white

layers

Tints of white—almost imperceptibly different—
create subtle shifts of atmosphere from room to room.

of white

IN AN ARTIST'S LIGHT-FILLED town house, the palette of the interior has been limited strictly to white. Tints in almost imperceptibly different variations—ranging from a pale chalky color to a slightly gray-green white—are used to cover every surface, including the floor. The very subtle shifts in shade that are seen from room to room and between the different surfaces make moving through these rooms a dynamic experience—much like traveling through a natural setting that contains a myriad of close-range colors.

The abundant natural light that floods the space allows this scheme to work very successfully. One feels that light itself is the color for these rooms, and in a way, it is. Since the white paints used here are pigmented

A chair draped in cotton canvas (RIGHT), melds with the all-white interior; against this background, colorful objects appear more intense, almost jewel-like. In the kitchen (PREVIOUS PAGE), soft morning light reflects the warmth of pale pine floors and wood chairs and mixes with the slight coolness of white walls to create a misty, shimmering atmosphere.

with a full spectrum of colors, all of the separate colors of light—red, yellow, blue, and violet—are emphasized as they are reflected. And because the tall windows of the house face east and west, the space receives the most beautiful light of the day, the soft light of early morning and the more golden cast of late afternoon.

In this collection of whites, the very slightest variation in the pigment mixture of the paints manipulates the interplay of the light from surface to surface. Some variations push the reflection toward a cool blue cast, others to a slight gray-green or a pale gold. Shadows seem to appear not as bleak grays, but are more like pale tints in a watercolor painting. In each

of these spare rooms, the shimmering effect caused by the interaction of close-range colors feels especially important here.

This reflective environment is kept vigorously simple; even the owner's paintings include collages of creamy white paper fixed to white canvas. The only colors that appear in furniture or objects are basic as well: black, the extreme comparison making the white whiter, and versions of the primaries, red, yellow, and blue.

It is a space that needs time to be fully appreciated, but even in a few minutes, the eye becomes adjusted to the subtle contrasts, and details soon evoke the same delicacy as elements in a misty landscape.

ABOVE: Thin gauze panels filter the subdued light of late afternoon, and it acquires a cool gray-green cast as walls are in shadow. A white-on-white canvas by Alexander Vethers hangs in the bedroom (RIGHT), a simple, tranquil space in which light reflected from the collection of full-spectrum whites seems to fill the space.

ocean

Colors taken from the seaside form the palette for two houses
near the ocean, creating a seamless extension of the setting.

light

THE INTERIOR of this small house near the ocean is a graceful expression of the natural qualities of the light inherent to its surroundings. Whites can appear even whiter with a touch of blue pigment, and can mimic the very pure white light reflected at a seaside location. Here the pale tints of color used are similar enough so that they visually blend together, evoking the atmospheric mist often seen near the ocean. The interior, designed by Benjamin Noriega-Ortiz, uses a very limited palette: white with enhancements of very light bleached wood and the palest hints of blue. This simple representation of sand, sea, and sky is not meant to draw attention to the architecture but to the surrounding atmosphere.

In this beach house, a range of pale accents visually blend together, providing subtle contrasts with the perimeter; blue notes actually seem to pull the sky inside. Windows are covered with cotton gauze shades that diffuse the soft light, creating its own variation of the misty atmosphere near the ocean.

Throughout the house, the presence of blue in the palette heightens the already abundant reflection of light, and the addition of blue accents to the rooms links the inside to its beach setting even more, as these blues seem to actually pull the sky in. The blue also complements the pale yellow of the natural wood, heightening its warmth and evoking the sand nearby. Though the effect of the blues in the interior is powerful, the actual colors are not intense; they are very pale and do not set up much of a contrast with the white walls. But even their very subtle contrast is significant, as it is felt in the luminous atmosphere their interplay provides. Gauzy window coverings in all of the rooms filter the light to further soften the contrasts.

Neither strong colors nor a wide variety of color is necessary here. In an oceanside setting such as this, the location itself is seen as a sanctuary; the house is simply an extension of the landscape. In this interior, the palette of sand, sea, and sky has literally been taken inside.

Light is filtered through windows and through airy linen slipcovers on the chairs. The interaction between close-range pale walls, floors, and furnishings creates a shimmering effect; blue pigments in the white lacquered dining table heighten the reflected light. As the eye adjusts to subtle contrasts of color, pale tints, such as the light blue of the cushions, become more intense.

ABOVE: Blue bed curtains complement the yellow tones of the natural wood wall and heighten its warmth. RIGHT: One strong contrast, a turquoise-blue rug, creates the sense of an oasis in a sitting room. Embroidered organdy covers a table (OPPOSITE), adding another texture and continuing the effect of filtered reflective light.

testing paint colors

WHEN CHOOSING a paint color for a room, there is no substitute for testing the color in the actual setting. Every space is unique, and everything from the quality of the light to the color of the floor will have an impact. If in selecting a color you are translating from a small chip to a fully painted room, keep in mind that the chip is not an accurate indication of how the color will appear when it fills the room. When the color is actually on the wall, it always appears much lighter and more intense (usually about twice as light and bright as the chip). So, to arrive at the color you want, try to choose a paint chip that seems twice as gray (or subdued) and twice as dark as you envision in the room.

making a test area

A TEST AREA has to be large to be effective—simply painting a few brushstrokes on a wall isn't enough. The bigger the test area, the more accurate your color projection will be. And, since it is difficult to choose color in a non-neutral room, try to make the environment for your test as neutral as possible. It's impossible to decide on a pale tint of green in a bright yellow room or subtly different whites in a red room; the reflected light from the stronger color will alter the perceived color in the test area. If the color of the room is too different from the range being tested it may be necessary to paint the space with white primer before the testing process begins. (Or you can cover the walls with paper, sheets, or drop cloths.) For the best viewing conditions, paint a swatch at least five feet wide from the floor to the ceiling, on a wall or walls opposite windows. If baseboards or crown molding will frame the wall color, it is helpful to paint them too.

primers and coverage

SINCE ALL PAINT is translucent, it takes more than one coat to provide complete coverage, even with light colors. All colors will perform best over white primer, as the white background bounces back any light that reaches it and keeps the desired color cleaner. Any other color added to the primer will affect the ultimate color of the finish paint. Even though using a tinted primer can make the job faster because it can mean fewer coats are required for coverage, always use as many coats of your finish color as necessary over a pure white background for both testing and finishing. It will result in the truest, cleanest final color.

reviewing the results

WITH THE TEST AREA painted, try to visualize the space by framing a view with your hands, blocking out the previous wall colors so you can see how the new color exists in the room. Try to envision the "world of the room" by incorporating as many elements as possible that will be included in the finished room: fabrics, carpets, furniture, and, most importantly, the floor.

Review the test at different times of the day to see how it reacts to changes in natural light or to artificial light at night. See if the color appears to be comfortable in the light in which it will be used most. A color that may be lovely by lamplight may appear too strong in bright sunlight.

making adjustments

DON'T BE SURPRISED if your paint color needs to be adjusted—toning down is often required. Depending on the color, a paint can usually be toned down by adding white or the color's complement, the color opposite it on a color wheel.

A too-bright red, for example, can be toned down with a touch of green. The very popular peach and apricot colors are flattering to most skin tones; they can create a wonderfully rich atmosphere and are especially beautiful in a candlelit dining room; however, they are easy to get wrong, and often end up too bright and one-dimensional. A touch of green will tone the brightness down. Blues, which can feel cold, may be surrounded with a warm frame, like cream trim, or yellow pigments can be added directly to the blue paint. If a green feels too cool, red, orange, or yellow can be added; in fact, any color will be warmed with red or yellow pigments.

If you need to adjust a paint color, any brand of universal colorants, available in all paint stores, are easy to use. Note and record how many drops of each pigment you add to a gallon of paint so that you can duplicate your color accurately. Proceed carefully—sometimes the tiniest amount of pigment is enough to significantly change the color.

selecting a finish

THE LUSTER, OR FINISH, of a paint can dramatically affect the way a completed room will look. Along with color, it is one of the important elements to be considered in the process of figuring out your space. Often, walls and ceilings are painted in a flat finish, with higher-gloss paints used for doors and detail work such as moldings. There are no hard-and-fast rules, however; it is a matter of personal preference—and what looks good to your eye in the space.

The best way to decide how flat or shiny your paint should be is to think about how you want the surface to appear. Paint with a flat finish is duller and will tend to make surfaces visually recede; more glossy paints appear brighter and harder and tend to visually advance. Generally speaking, the flatter the finish, the greater the illusion of depth. Especially in a flat paint with full-spectrum pigmentation, there is a feeling of a dematerialized surface, a softer plane whose exact distance from your eye is difficult to determine. This visual fuzziness seats walls and ceilings in the background, and they appear more as misty atmospheres than solid barriers. With higher-gloss paints, surfaces become visually harder. A shinier

finish is often appropriate for window or door frames and emphasizes the difference between their structural purpose and the adjoining plaster walls. Flat paint can make a decorative crown molding, regardless of its material, look more plasterlike and reveal more delicate detail.

High gloss paint is a great luxury, requiring the most preparation and application time. But surprisingly, it can be an exception to the "flatter the finish, the greater the depth" rule. By bouncing so much light off its surface, high gloss can create its own variety of ambiguity and depth. Depending on the setting, it may also be an effective way to disguise an imperfect surface. Between these two extremes, it is usually safer to stay as close to flat on walls and ceilings as practical considerations allow.

For woodwork and trim, higher-sheen products are problematic: Oils or alkyds (solvent-based) can be brushed out smooth, but will yellow over time; acrylics or latexes (water-based) dry too fast to level out and, when viewed up close, show plastic-looking textures of brush or roller marks. In general, eggshell, pearl, and satin are sheens that will wear well and look good.

Choosing the right finish can be confusing since labels on paint cans often don't reflect the actual finish. "Eggshell" and "satin," for example—words that are intrinsically appealing—are often incorrectly used. Below is a listing of kinds of finishes in order of increasing shininess.

Matte or flat enamel	Satin or soft gloss
Eggshell, low-luster, or angular sheen	Semigloss
Pearl	Gloss, high gloss, and/or lacquer

palette guide

This is a guide for using the paints from The Donald Kaufman Color Collection to create the palettes shown in this book or your own variations. For information about paints and color swatches from The Collection call 1-800-977-9198.

Some of the palettes created by individual home owners are also included as examples of additional ranges. Colors not available from The Collection are indicated by asterisks (*).

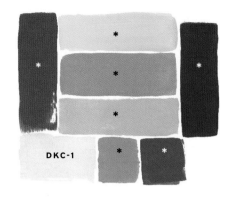

page 16

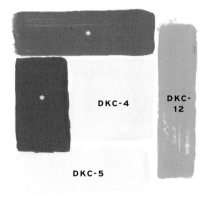

page 22

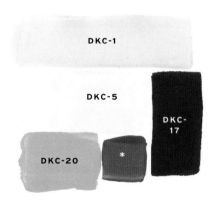

page 30

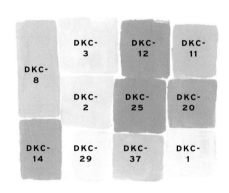

page 40

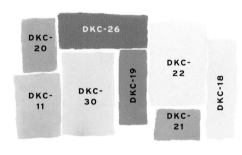

page 46

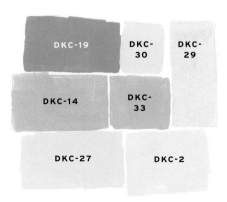

page 52

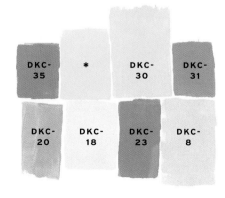

page 60

page 68

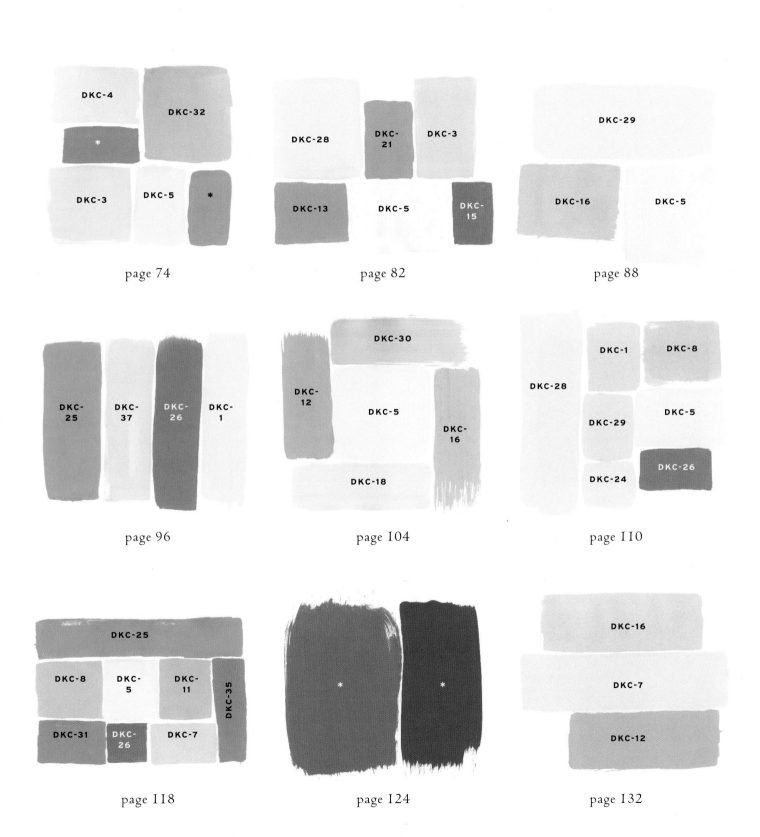

DKC-4

DKC-32

*

DKC-3   DKC-5   *

page 74

DKC-28   DKC-21   DKC-3

DKC-13   DKC-5   DKC-15

page 82

DKC-29

DKC-16   DKC-5

page 88

DKC-25   DKC-37   DKC-26   DKC-1

page 96

DKC-30

DKC-12   DKC-5   DKC-16

DKC-18

page 104

DKC-28   DKC-1   DKC-8

DKC-29   DKC-5

DKC-24   DKC-26

page 110

DKC-25

DKC-8   DKC-5   DKC-11   DKC-35

DKC-31   DKC-26   DKC-7

page 118

*   *

page 124

DKC-16

DKC-7

DKC-12

page 132

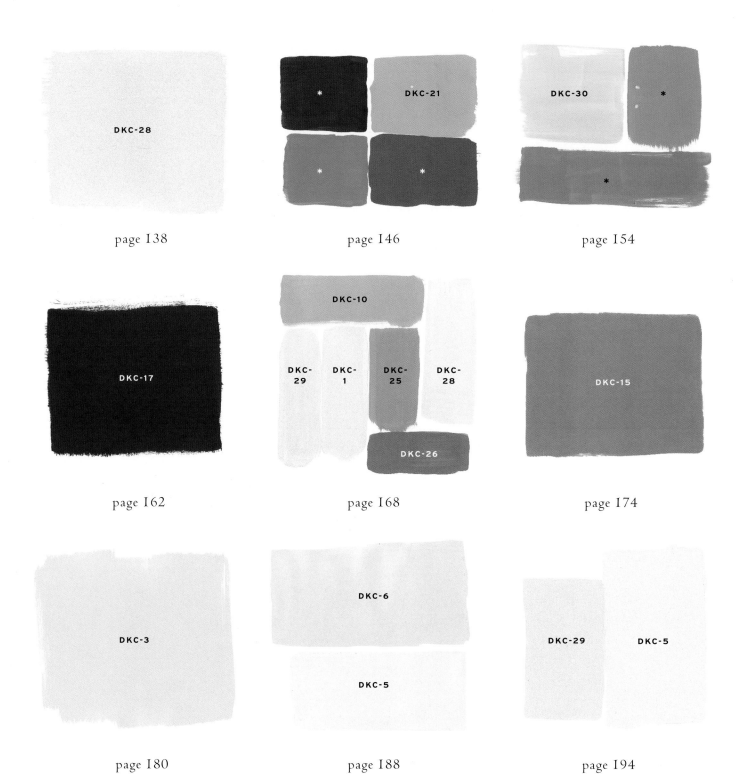